Original title:
Stalks of Serenity

Copyright © 2025 Creative Arts Management OÜ
All rights reserved.

Author: Liam Sterling
ISBN HARDBACK: 978-1-80567-048-3
ISBN PAPERBACK: 978-1-80567-128-2

The Dance of Sunlight and Shadow

In the garden, light does prance,
As shadows try to steal a chance.
A leaf spins round, with glee it twirls,
While beetles host their wiggly whirls.

The sun's a jester, glints and glows,
While flowers laugh in bright, weird clothes.
The breeze joins in, a playful tease,
As nature's joy puts hearts at ease.

Resting in Nature's Embrace

Lying down in grass so bright,
I swear it tickles, what a sight!
A butterfly lands on my nose,
And giggles while my laughter grows.

The trees above start a loud chat,
With squirrels shouting, "What of that?"
While worms below dance disco style,
I can't help but grin, it's all worthwhile!

Silent Symphony of Green

In the forest, a quiet choir,
From rustling leaves to ants that aspire.
A frog sings bass, a bird takes lead,
While trees sway softly, dancing with speed.

The grasshoppers leap with perfect flair,
While caterpillars munch without a care.
The melody's sweet, though slightly bizarre,
Nature's humor shines like a shooting star.

Murmurs of a Gentle Stream

A stream flows by, it murmurs tales,
Of fish that swim and ducks with sails.
It giggles, splashes, what a tease,
While pebbles chuckle in the breeze.

Tiny frogs leap with joyful glee,
While dragonflies buzz, all carefree.
The water winks, "Don't take me seriously,"
As ripples laugh in pure deliriously!

Tranquil Breezes at Dawn

Silence greets the morning sun,
As squirrels play and have their fun.
The coffee brews, a joyful tease,
While birds perform their morning sneeze.

Wind whispers secrets to the leaves,
A dance of joy, oh how it weaves.
The cat just naps, its dreams are bright,
As gnomes giggle in morning light.

Petals of Peace

Flowers bloom with silly faces,
Tickling bees in funny places.
A butterfly flies with grace and flair,
Daring the snail to a race with air.

Ladybugs laugh, they twirl and spin,
While a worm jokes about his skin.
In this garden, joy is found,
Where even dirt is soft and sound.

Threads of Stillness

In quiet corners, spiders weave,
Funny tales that will deceive.
They spin their webs with twists and grins,
While the goldfish flaunt their fins.

A frog croaks out a silly tune,
To entertain the lazy moon.
Each quiet spot a burst of cheer,
Where giggles dance, we hold them dear.

Harmony in the Hush

Underneath a shady tree,
A sloth is zipping, can you see?
His slow-mo moves bring laughter loud,
As ants march by, all very proud.

The wind picks up a feather's flight,
And pelicans joke, oh what a sight!
In whispered tones, the critters crack,
A symphony we can't take back.

Seraphic Sounds of the Forest

In the woods where squirrels play,
A symphony of chirps all day.
The trees dance with breezy cheer,
While raccoons drink their roots of beer.

The owls hoot with comic flair,
As mushrooms giggle, unaware.
The branches sway, they sing and tease,
While ants march on like tiny wheeze.

Each leaf whispers jokes to the sun,
A punchline found in every run.
The colors laugh in vibrant hues,
Combined in nature's funny views.

So if you wander through this space,
Expect a chuckle, a warm embrace.
The forest speaks in quirky ways,
Tickling hearts in endless plays.

Midnight Murmurs

When shadows stretch and crickets croon,
The moonlight dances, making tunes.
A raccoon in a top hat prances,
While fireflies take their glowing chances.

The owls are gossiping all night,
Trading tales in the silver light.
With laughter echoing far and wide,
A chorus that no one can bide.

Beneath the stars, the night bumbles,
As dreams take shape and silence fumbles.
Whispers float on soft, cool air,
Like secrets shared without a care.

So if you hear the midnight speak,
Stick around; it's fun, not bleak.
With every noise, a chuckle blooms,
In shadowy corners, laughter looms.

The Language of Quiet Spaces

In corners where the stillness lies,
A decibel of giggles arises.
Dust bunnies have a silent race,
While shadows trade a soft embrace.

Each muffled sound, a secret code,
In cozy nooks where whispers flowed.
A butterfly sneezes, strange and grand,
Tickling petals with a gentle hand.

The clocks snicker at passing time,
As sleepy cats drop in a rhyme.
Every echo shares a jest,
A quiet laugh, a charming quest.

In tranquil spots where stillness reigns,
The world spins on in playful chains.
Listen close, and you just might,
Unravel laughter tucked in the night.

Dreaming in Soft Greens

In the meadow's embrace, a gentle spree,
Where daisies sway and dance with glee.
A frog in a crown, quite the sight,
Chasing butterflies into the night.

The grass tickles toes as you stroll,
While ants recite their marching roll.
The daisies nod with sunny grace,
In this jester's garden, find your place.

High above, the clouds play hide and seek,
While laughter blooms, a gentle peak.
A breeze slips by with a chuckle sweet,
Enticing you with nature's beat.

So wander deep in hues of green,
Where fun and joy are often seen.
In every step, a giggle waits,
As nature spins its playful fates.

Every Step a Prayer

With every step I take, a joke,
I trip on roots, oh what a hoax!
The grass it laughs beneath my shoes,
A dance of faith, in silly blues.

My feet they shuffle like a song,
Creating tunes where I belong.
The squirrels cheer, they find it grand,
As I lead a merry, wobbly band.

Each stumble's just a little prayer,
For grace to guide me through the air.
The daisies giggle, bloom and sway,
As I parade in goofy fray.

So let me slip, let me collide,
In laughter's grace, I take my stride.
With joy beneath, my heart, a flare,
Each step I take, a prayer, I swear!

The Beauty of Unbroken Silence

In the hush where whispers play,
The grass decides to steal the day.
The crickets chirp a quiet tune,
While ants don hats and dance in June.

With stillness comes the comic plight,
A squirrel sneezes, oh what a sight!
The flowers nod with cheer and flair,
In unbroken silence, there's much to share.

I tiptoe through this space divine,
Where every leaf becomes a sign.
The wind, it giggles, whoosh and sway,
Making quiet giggles, come what may.

So here I sit, with nature's jest,
In peaceful laughs, I find my rest.
For in the calm, the truth prevails,
The beauty found in silent tales.

Sheltered from the Clamor

In a cozy nook, away from noise,
I snuggle up with my quirky toys.
The world outside may blare and shout,
But here, fun reigns; there's no doubt.

A turtle peeks, it needs a break,
While nearby frogs do bellyache.
The whispers of the leaves around,
Create a hush, a wicked sound.

With laughter loud, I sip my tea,
The beetles join in harmony.
Together we make merry cheer,
In a sheltered dance, we've nothing to fear.

So here's to quiet, where I can rest,
In joyful silence, I am blessed.
Clamor outside? Not a treasure,
In my world of fun, I find my pleasure!

The Essence of Emptiness

In empty space, a crazed balloon,
It floats on by, a jesting noon.
The void's a canvas, white and bare,
Where even whispers try to flare.

With nothing here, my mind takes flight,
To ponder jokes in pure delight.
The echo of my laughter thrums,
As shadows dance like ticklish chums.

A space that's full, yet also bare,
Is where I find my silly stare.
For emptiness, oh what a tease,
Makes room for laughter, joy, and ease.

So let the quiet be my stage,
In this grand void, I engage.
The essence lost, yet found today,
In moments where we laugh and play!

A Tapestry of Rustling Foliage

Leaves dance like clowns in the breeze,
Whispering secrets and tickling trees.
Squirrels in costumes, acorns in hand,
Hosting a party across the green land.

Amidst the rustle, a frog plays the lute,
A deer in a tutu, it's quite a hoot!
All nature chuckles, no reason to frown,
In this leafy circus, let joy come around.

Canvas of the Contemplative Heart

A snail's slow race, just taking its time,
While a grasshopper croaks his own silly rhyme.
Butterflies prance wearing shirts made of light,
Taking life easy, all day and all night.

The clouds float by, in a dance of delight,
Casting shapes of laughter, oh what a sight!
With a wink and a grin, the earth joins the fun,
Painting a picture where happiness runs.

Caress of the Morning Mist

The mist tiptoes in with a giggle so soft,
Wrapping the world in a blanket aloft.
It plays peek-a-boo, then suddenly swells,
Hiding the rabbits, oh what a tale it tells!

A rooster crows loudly, "Where's my toast, dear?"
While a cat rolls in droplets, shedding a tear.
The sun blinks awake, gives a yawn and a stretch,
And the day begins with laughter to fetch.

Reverie Among the Wildflowers

In fields of color, a bee sings along,
Mixing up pollen like a confused chef's song.
A butterfly winks, says, "Aren't I a sight?"
While daisies giggle, basking in the light.

Tickled by daisies, a bumblebee twirls,
Taking a break from his busy world.
Laughing together, the flowers all sway,
In a funny dance that brightens the day.

Serenity's Hidden Corners

In a garden where laughter blooms,
Worms dance like stars in dust-filled rooms.
A gnome with a hat that's askew, oh my!
Is he plotting a garden party pie?

Bees wear sunglasses, they're feeling cool,
Butterflies play hopscotch on the pool.
Even the daisies chuckle and sway,
As the sun sprays gold on an ordinary day.

A cat naps inside a flower pot,
Dreaming of fish, or maybe not.
The wind whispers secrets in a breeze,
While squirrels laugh at their own unease.

In these corners, joy is the find,
Laughter splashes, and woes unwind.
While the world rushes, we savor this bliss,
In the quirky embrace of nature's kiss.

The Silence Between Heartbeats

Tick-tock trips with a silly hop,
Time wears a clown wig, never will stop.
Between the beats, there's giggling space,
Where socks disappear with a jester's grace.

A turtle's slow dance moves crickets to cheer,
As ants throw a party with snacks aplenty here.
The heartbeat of nature is comically slow,
Like a snail who thinks he's the star of the show.

In this silence, mischief brews bright,
Bubbles of laughter pop day and night.
The stars in the sky wink with delight,
As fireflies join in a twinkling fight.

So embrace the quiet, the whimsical hush,
Let's laugh at the simple, no need for a rush.
From pulse to pulse, let's find our glee,
In moments that tickle, just you and me.

Embracing Nature's Quiet Wisdom

A wise old tree with a beard of moss,
Is sharing secrets without a gloss.
Squirrels gather 'round, so attentive and bold,
Hanging on tales that never grow old.

Grass blades gossip when the wind runs wild,
And flowers nod in harmony, happy and mild.
A wiggly worm has a story or two,
About the great rain that splashed in the dew.

The clouds, they chuckle, not taking a stand,
A spontaneous shower, now isn't that grand?
The puddles reflect a jester's hot air,
While frogs leap for joy – who can really care?

In every whisper, there's wisdom we glean,
Amidst the giggles of the unseen.
Let's learn from nature with a wink and a grin,
In her playful embrace, let the fun begin!

A Sanctuary for the Soul

In a meadow where butterflies tell jokes,
Joy blooms like flowers, amusing the folks.
Nestled beneath a pancake-shaped cloud,
A picnic of laughter, we gather so loud.

The breeze tickles trees, a soft caress,
Whispering secrets, a natural mess.
Nestlings giggle in nests made of twine,
As the daisies gossip, "Look, he's divine!"

Bobbling along, the brook sings a song,
Stepping stones giggle as we hop along.
Nature's a jester, with colors so bright,
Painting smiles under the golden daylight.

In this sanctuary, worries just fade,
With laughter and mischief, joyfully laid.
So let's twirl together, in nature's embrace,
In this wondrous escape, we all find our place.

Blossoms in the Embrace of Time

In a garden where giggles bloom,
Flowers wear hats, like they own the room.
Bouncing bees dance in a silly jig,
Sipping sweet nectar, feeling quite big.

A snail on a mission, slow but bold,
Dreams of a sprint; oh, stories told!
Roses giggle as they sway with grace,
While daisies gossip about the missing vase.

The sun winks down with a cheerful grin,
While thorns complain, 'We never win!'
Yet amidst the laughter and the playful sprigs,
Life blooms with joy, making us all figs.

So let's tiptoe through this blossomed spree,
Humming silly tunes, just you and me.
For in this wild patch where antics align,
We find our roots in the arms of time.

Soft Shadows of a Dusk's Promise

In twilight's realm where shadows tease,
Mice in tuxedos dance with ease.
The moon looks down with a cheeky flair,
While crickets chatter like they just don't care.

The trees whisper secrets, heavy with glee,
As owls hoot wisdom, but drink too much tea.
Frogs in tuxes croak a merry tune,
While fireflies flash like stars gone balloon.

A breeze sways gently, tickling grass,
While the sun sets quietly, letting shadows pass.
With each chuckle shared, dusk holds tight,
A promise of laughter, within the night.

So come join the fun as the colors blend,
Where silliness whispers around every bend.
For even in shadows, the joy will arise,
In this playful dusk, where laughter fills the skies.

The Harmony of Nature's Cradle

In the cradle of leaves where laughter flows,
Squirrels wear shades as the laughter grows.
Birds in a choir sing off-key tunes,
While nature chuckles at the silly prunes.

A caterpillar's joke gets a forest-wide cheer,
While frogs ribbit tales that we all want to hear.
Buzzy bees buzzing a comical tune,
Nectar so sweet, they dance like a cartoon.

The flowers wiggle in a colorful dance,
Dandelions issue spontaneous prance.
Laughter erupts as a butterfly slips,
Flip-flopping through petals, taking odd trips.

Nature sings loud, in a giggly embrace,
With each rustle and giggle, it finds its place.
So let's join this harmony, wild and untamed,
In a world where joy is forever proclaimed.

Light Filtering Through Woven Dreams

Through cracks in the trees, the sunlight peeks,
Casting goofy shadows, making us peak.
The breeze gently teases, with a playful call,
While butterflies giggle, hoping not to fall.

In a patchwork of rays, laughter unfolds,
A rabbit in shades, doing tricks bold.
Each flicker of light like a tickling hand,
As squirrels conspire to make the day grand.

Frolicking friends in a radiant dance,
Chasing the glimmers, lost in a trance.
With each twinkling ray, more giggles are found,
In this woven dream, where joy doth abound.

So let us bask in this warm, gleeful glow,
Where laughter is endless, and wonders bestow.
For light filters softly, painting us free,
In a world full of chuckles, just you and me.

The Calm After the Storm

The clouds have fled, what a sight,
Leaves are dancing, feeling light.
I slipped on mud, oh what a scene,
Nature giggles, a quiet queen.

Raindrops linger on a twig,
Raccoons waddle with a jig.
I laugh at thunder, what a tease,
Dancing squirrels, if you please!

Reflections in a Still Pool

The water's calm, a mirror's grin,
Frogs hop by with a cheeky spin.
My face swims up, oh what a blunder,
A fish just winked, chaos or wonder?

The dragonflies play peek-a-boo,
As I splash back, quite the view.
Count my toes, then a belly flop,
Nature's chuckle, I just can't stop!

The Solace of Whispering Pines

Amidst the trees, whispers flirt,
Pine needles fall, a playful spurt.
A squirrel darts, with nuts to hoard,
I trip on roots, common concord.

The whispers giggle, a secret spree,
I shout back loud, they laugh at me.
Got lost in thoughts of pinecone hats,
The pines just shrug, 'We're not your mats!'

Nature's Gentle Caress

The sun peeks in with a golden grin,
Bumblebees dance, let the fun begin.
I swat a bug, a comical fight,
Mother Nature claims, 'You're not my knight!'

Petals flutter, the breeze is aloof,
I chase butterflies, feeling the goof.
Laying on grass, I spot a cloud,
It's a rabbit! Staring back, oh so proud!

Streams of Quiet Beauty

In a meadow where the grass does sway,
A rabbit hops and wins the day.
He tripped on roots, oh what a sight,
Then danced away in pure delight.

Butterflies tease him, flit and glide,
They giggle as he tries to hide.
A ladybug joins, sounds like a cheer,
"Come join our fun, you silly dear!"

With each tumble, laughter does bloom,
Even flowers join the playful room.
They raise their petals in a wave,
For the joy that nature gave.

So under skies of azure hue,
The silly rabbit just laughs anew.
Life's a party in the grass,
And each little critter's got sass.

Under the Canopy of Peace

Beneath the branches, life takes a nap,
Squirrels juggle acorns without a flap.
A sleepy deer snorts, "What's all this fuss?"
While frogs croak loud, like a raucous bus.

The breeze whispers secrets to the trees,
While bees in their buzz, aim for some cheese.
"Why cheese?" asks a squirrel, with a smirk,
"No idea," replies the bee, "Just a perk!"

A bear reworks his yoga pose,
Stuck in downward dog, he strikes a rose.
The raccoons clap, cheering for style,
"A round of applause, he's flexible by a mile!"

Smiles abound in this woodsy retreat,
Where laughter and calm in nature meet.
Under this canopy with such great zest,
Every creature feels truly blessed.

Soft Lullabies of the Wild

Night falls softly, stars begin to twink,
A hedgehog hums, but the moths will wink.
"Shhh, you're startling my snooze!" one cries,
While crickets chime in with soft lullabies.

A sleepy owl hoots, "Not too loud, my dears!"
"I'm counting sheep, oh look, three cheers!"
The raccoons giggle, their hush now broken,
"Who knew the night was so funny, unspoken!"

From bushes and trees, the insects join in,
A chorus of sounds, like joy on a whim.
They tickle the night with a whimsical cheer,
As woodland animals cuddle, feeling near.

So snuggle with giggles in this vibrant dream,
The wild hums softly, sewing a seam.
In this humorous hush, sleep comes to play,
As nature herself folds the night away.

A Journey into the Quiet

Adventure calls, grab your gear,
A snail shouts, "I'm ready, oh dear!"
With a shell so heavy yet heart so light,
He's off to explore in the fading night.

He meets a toad with a musical croak,
"Hop on my back for a taste of the joke!"
Together they glide past twinkling dew,
While the moon winks down, illuminating the view.

A breeze gusts wildly, tickles their nose,
Making the pals giggle, and that's how it goes.
"Onward!" yells the toad, looking quite grand,
While snails pull up pace, as fast as they can!

The night wraps them in a soft, silly hug,
Promising stories, like a cozy drug.
In their journey through quiet, laughter they seek,
Finding joy in the simple, that's the peak!

Footprints on Soft Earth

In a field where laughter grows,
I left my shoes, but where they goes?
A rabbit claimed them for a race,
Now I wear a sock's embrace.

The daisies giggle, tickle my toes,
While ants march by in fancy clothes.
They say I'm lost, oh what a sight,
Dancing with shadows in broad daylight.

My thoughts drift off like kites in the breeze,
Chasing butterflies with utmost ease.
Even clouds wink as they float by,
Who knew serenity could be so spry?

Yet, here I stand with feet in mud,
Swapping stories with a friendly bud.
With each laugh, my heart takes flight,
Who needs shoes when joy feels right?

Traces of a Wandering Mind

In a garden full of thought and jest,
My mind took off, it liked the quest.
It jumped on leaves and danced on grass,
While I just sat, a kindly ass.

A squirrel ran by and tossed a wink,
Curious minds — what do they think?
Maybe they ponder nuts and cheese,
While I muse on worlds with ease.

Thoughts twirl round like chips on a plate,
I chase them down, but they just skate.
Oh, for a net to catch a dream,
But they flee like the shyest beam.

So I sit here, sipping frisky tea,
With scattered thoughts surrounding me.
Wandering minds, what a wild thrill,
Just don't forget to pay the bill!

In the Shade of Dreams

Under a tree where nonsense reigns,
I chase my thoughts like runaway trains.
A nap sounds sweet, but dreams won't share,
They dance around without a care.

The shadows play hide and seek with sun,
While I've misplaced the last 'just for fun'.
Can I borrow a giggle from the wind?
Or will it stick to roots unpinned?

A squirrel recites a poem to the sky,
I applaud in silence, oh my, oh my!
The sun nods off beneath some clouds,
While I make jokes to invisible crowds.

So here I lounge, in this soft retreat,
With every whim, my day feels neat.
Dreams laugh along and I can't complain,
In this shade, I find my playful lane!

Embracing the Quietude

In a cozy nook where whispers nest,
I wear a smile, it's the silliest quest.
A cat yawns out an echoing cheer,
While I pretend that it's all very clear.

Clouds float by like marshmallows sweet,
They'd be perfect for a whimsical treat!
But I just sip from my empty cup,
As ideas swirl, I raise them up.

Embracing silence, I stifle my giggles,
While bugs on walls are doing their wiggles.
Here tranquility gives me the plot,
Where humor and peace stir in a pot.

With every chuckle, serenity grows,
In a world that dances, all joys expose.
Rain may drop, but I won't pout,
For laughter's an umbrella I carry about!

Echoes of Old Growth

In the woods, trees chat and boast,
Their ancient tales, we love the most.
Squirrels giggle, acorns they toss,
While branches dance, with a playful gloss.

Mossy rugs invite a nap,
While chirping birds set the trap.
Why worry 'bout the busy grind?
Here, laughter's the treasure we find.

Leaves whisper secrets of the past,
While fungi dress up for a feast so vast.
The roots below wiggle with glee,
As bushy tails mock the bumblebee.

Nature grins with an earnest tease,
Tickling us with a gentle breeze.
Among the giants, we feel so small,
Yet laugh out loud, we're having a ball.

Nature's Gentle Coda

In gardens lush, where veggies play,
The tomatoes dance in bright array.
Cucumbers whisper in silly lines,
While peppers throw colorful signs.

Sunflowers wave with big, bright smiles,
Winking at bugs in floral styles.
Bees buzz jokes we can't quite grasp,
Yet join the fun, the joy feels vast.

A rabbit hops, it steals a bite,
While carrots giggle at the sight.
Chickens cluck with comedic flair,
As if they were on stage, so rare.

Nature's laughter echoes wide,
In this world, we must abide.
So grab your hat and join the fun,
The earth's a stage, for everyone.

In Pursuit of Inner Tranquility

On a quest for peace, we sneak and peek,
Through tangled paths, the view is unique.
A frog leaps by, croaking a tune,
While crickets join in, under the moon.

The river chuckles, bubbles abound,
Secrets and whispers twirl all around.
With rocks that giggle, and willows that sway,
Nature's a joker, come out and play.

Finding stillness in cheeky ways,
As foxes prance through their woodland ballet.
The calm we seek, it hides in the fun,
Where peace and laughter dance as one.

So lose the frown and chase the delight,
For joy is the path that feels just right.
With every step, a chuckle will greet,
On our journey to find the serene beat.

Woven Dreams of Dappled Sunlight

In dappled light, where shadows play,
Dreams of mischief prance all day.
Butterflies twirl in colors bright,
Making petals giggle, what a sight!

The sun peeks through, a cheeky grin,
While ants in line march with a spin.
A spider spins webs of laughter and grace,
Each thread a joy, each knot a race.

Clouds drift by, in shapes so silly,
Turning frowns into a thrill, oh really?
With breezy whispers, trees throw shade,
Inviting all to join the charade.

So bask in mirth, in golden rays,
Dancing with whims, in playful ways.
Where sunlight weaves a funny dream,
Nature's giggle is the sweetest theme.

The Lullaby of Leaves

In the breeze, leaves dance and twirl,
A squirrel drops acorns with a whirl.
The branches swing, a leafy band,
As nature plays its funny hand.

The robin hums a cheeky song,
While ants parade, all marching strong.
With tiny hats and shoes so bright,
They steal the show, what a delight!

A caterpillar takes a nap,
On a leaf, it makes a map.
Dreaming of wings and skies so blue,
In funny dreams, it sways askew.

The breeze whispers jokes through the trees,
With chuckles shared by bumblebees.
Nature's humor, oh so sly,
Every leaf laughs as they fly high.

Beneath the Quiet Canopy

Underneath the leafy shade,
A turtle plays, but is delayed.
He wears a shell that's quite a sight,
And laughs at shadows in the light.

A bunny hops, with quite a leap,
As if he's trying to dance and sweep.
His floppy ears go left and right,
Making friends with the mushrooms bright.

The crickets chirp a symphony,
Old jokes that only they can see.
In the hush of emerald trees,
Laughter swirls among the leaves.

With sunlight filtering through the green,
Silly moments, sights unseen.
A woodpecker plays a drum so well,
Telling tales that swell and swell.

Blossoms of Contentment

Petals giggle as they unfold,
In colors bright, both bold and gold.
The daisies gossip in the sun,
While bees bring nectar, just for fun.

A butterfly flutters with flair,
Making sure no one's unaware.
With polka dots and stripes so loud,
She prances through her blooming crowd.

The sunflowers nod, with laughter deep,
As shadows play, they twist and creep.
While turtles yawn, and stretch so wide,
In blossoms' joy, they take great pride.

In this garden, joyous and bright,
Nature's comedy, pure delight.
Each whisper, chuckle, every cheer,
In this bloom, happiness draws near.

Serene Silhouettes at Twilight

As twilight draws its curtain low,
The fireflies start their funny show.
They glow like stars on a cosmic spree,
Dancing wildly, oh what glee!

The owls hoot jokes in muffled tones,
As shadows gather with playful groans.
With moonbeams throwing silver light,
Each creature winks in the night's invite.

A raccoon sneaks with a little grin,
Trying to find where dreams begin.
His clever paws are deft and sly,
As he nabs some crumbs with a quick dash by.

The night wraps all in a gentle hug,
While laughter bubbles like a cozy mug.
In serene silhouettes, tones of cheer,
Nature whispers a giggle to our ear.

Echoes from the Glade

In the glade where whispers sing,
A squirrel's dance is quite the thing.
Tree trunks giggle, roots delight,
With every rustle, sparks ignite.

The frogs croak jokes, who knew they'd be
Stand-up stars in nature's spree?
A butterfly lost, can't find its way,
Winks at the sun, then hides till it's gray.

Mice run races, tails a-blur,
While owls hoot, "Cat got your fur?"
A picnic's spread on a blanket of grass,
With ants queuing up for a little mass.

In this glade where laughter grows,
Even the lichens tell some prose.
So come and sit in this zany spot,
Where every oak's a favorite lot.

Floating on a Sea of Stillness

Leaves drift down like clumsy boats,
While frogs in boats wear funny coats.
A breeze tickles every green face,
And nature giggles, finding its place.

Clouds above play hide and seek,
As geese pass by, all fowl and cheek.
An old stone gnome chuckles in jest,
"I'm more stylish than the birds in their nest!"

A fish jumps up, does a flip,
Splashing around, it takes a dip.
The moon peeks down, winks at the pond,
Who knew stillness could be so fond?

In quiet corners, silliness reigns,
With turtles spinning in happy chains.
Let's float on this calm, let laughter ring,
In this haven of giggles, let us swing!

Harmony of the Hidden Grove

In the grove where secrets hide,
A raccoon wears a cloak of pride.
Squirrels gossip, nuts in hand,
With every crack, the jokes expand.

See the brown bear dance away,
While bees zoom 'round in a funny ballet.
The cacti chuckle, arms out wide,
"Don't come too close; we're tough to bide!"

Beneath the boughs, a rabbit slips,
Chasing shadows, it does flips.
With mushrooms laughing, "What a show!"
Tiny creatures share tales that flow.

A harmony brewed in this grove so tight,
Where dawn meets dusk in pure delight.
Nature's orchestra plays the tunes,
Of whimsy and joy beneath the moons.

The Poetry of Falling Leaves

As leaves drop down, a paper dance,
They swirl and twirl, each step a chance.
Acorns roll like tiny drums,
And nature's laughter softly hums.

A leaf decides to take a ride,
On a busy squirrel, full of pride.
Together they plot a daring scheme,
To join the clouds, to live the dream.

The wind plays tricks, tugs at their shoes,
While trees shout out, "No time to snooze!"
Down below, a raccoon spies,
Jokes to share, and friendly whys.

So gather 'round for tales of gold,
Nature's slapstick, never old.
In every flutter, find your glee,
In the poetry of the falling spree.

A Symphony of Unseen Wings

A duck in a tux, playing the flute,
Makes all of the flowers dance and hoot.
The cat joins the band, with a tambourine,
While a squirrel leads the charge, so keen.

A bee sings a tune, buzzes with glee,
Jiving with daisies, what a sight to see!
The sun starts to giggle, rolling on by,
As the rabbits are hopping, oh my oh my!

A snail on a skateboard zooms on the track,
While a frog does ballet with a style he won't lack.
The butterfly chorus flutters in tune,
As the garden goes wild, beneath the bright moon.

Laughter spills gently, like raindrops on leaves,
In a world where the ordinary weaves.
So come join the fun, as the day softly sings,
In a symphony sweet with unseen wings.

Fragrance of Dawn's Embrace

The coffee pot wheezes, a morning delight,
With pancakes that dance, it's quite the sight.
A cat in a beret critiques the toast,
While the dog in sunglasses is bragging the most.

The sun yawns awake, stretching its beams,
As waffles pop up, like sweet little dreams.
Behind the curtain, a sock puppet cheers,
"More syrup, please!" it squeaks, with no fears.

The flowers are plotting, attempting to bloom,
While a hedgehog's sneezing creates quite the room.
The breeze whispers secrets to each dainty rose,
As the morning unfolds in its comical prose.

With giggles and grumbles, the day finds its pace,
As breakfast assembles in a harmonious race.
So raise up your forks, let the laughter embrace,
In the fragrance of dawn, every smile finds its place.

The Stillness Between Heartbeats

A frog with a top hat dances on logs,
While turtles play poker, disguised as their dogs.
In the stillness of moments, a giggle unfolds,
As the beetles tell jokes, each sillier than told.

A heartbeat is whispered, then tickles the air,
While a squirrel juggles acorns without a care.
The silence is golden, yet laughter runs free,
As the owls roll their eyes, sipping tea with glee.

Of moments unspoken, a squeak and a sigh,
Where the waves of a breeze whisper laughter nearby.
The clock ticks in rhythm, but we dance in delight,
In the stillness that blossoms as day turns to night.

With a jump and a shuffle, the joy intertwines,
In the spaces unfilled, where the silliness shines.
Embrace every heartbeat, let humor take flight,
In the harmony sweet of the day turning bright.

In the Arms of Gentle Whispers

A secretive shadow plays hide and seek,
Where the tulips gossip and the daisies speak.
With whispers of giggles beneath the soft trees,
A fox in a tutu sways with the breeze.

In a world where the winds chuckle in rhyme,
The ants plan a picnic, but run out of time!
A snail's slow salsa sets the mood just right,
As the fireflies twinkle, igniting the night.

The frogs wear their capes, ready for flight,
While the owls recite poetry under moonlight.
The echoes of laughter float soft on the air,
In the arms of sweet whispers, we gather, we share.

So let's twirl with the petals, spin 'round with the stars,
As the laughter encircles with rather no bars.
For in every soft secret that nature will find,
Is a spark of pure joy that can tickle the mind.

Echoes of Gentle Breezes

The whispers float on air like jokes,
A cheeky breeze that pokes and prods.
It tickles petals, makes them laugh,
A fluttering dance with nature's nods.

Leaves giggle as they sway and twirl,
While branches chuckle with delight.
The flowers gossip, spilling tea,
In hues of laughter, oh what a sight!

Even the clouds wear sly grins,
As shadows play tag on the ground.
The sun beams down, a goofy friend,
Sharing humor all around.

Oh, how the world can be a jest,
With nature's comedy to unfold.
Each gentle gust a punchline shared,
In this landscape soft and bold.

The Dance of Silent Leaves

Leaves prance about on playful knees,
Trying hard not to cause a fuss.
Yet when the gusts give them a tease,
They trip and fall, all in a rush.

Their laughter rustles in the air,
As branches sway in matching tune.
A waltz with chirping birds to share,
Beneath a chuckling afternoon.

Here comes a squirrel, with acorn stash,
Dancing to a rhythm of its own.
With every leap and bounding dash,
It's clear he sets the world to groan.

So let them swirl, both bold and brave,
In nature's merry cavalcade.
Life's a stage where all can play,
In this leafy, lively charade.

Hushed Conversations in the Meadow

In the meadow, grasses meet,
They whisper secrets soft and light.
Each blade sways to a rhythm sweet,
As ladybugs join in the delight.

Bees giggle as they hum their tune,
Pollinating plans of blissful cheer.
While daisies plot a grand festoon,
Adorning the ground with floral gear.

The breeze brings chuckles from afar,
A breeze who teases all it sees.
Echoes of laughter, like a star,
Tickle the memories of the trees.

So hush your noise and listen close,
To nature's jokes, a tender sound.
In this meadow, joy can't dose,
As laughter roams the green around.

Lullabies of the Winding Path

A winding path that twists and curves,
Invites us in with smiles wide.
Every stone and pebble serves
As a punchline in this joyride.

The trees lean in to catch the tale,
Of travelers with shoes untied.
They chuckle softly, "Please don't fail,
And trip on roots you can't abide!"

With each step, a new jest unfolds,
As flowers brighten with their cheer.
Even tired feet can lift their soles,
When surrounded by such blissful spheres.

So walk the path, let laughter start,
With every twist, a playful sing.
In the embrace of nature's heart,
Life's a giggle, let freedom ring!

In the Heart of Stillness

In the garden, quiet and bright,
A snail races, oh what a sight!
With a helmet made of lettuce leaves,
It's the grand prix of garden thieves!

Butterflies dance with the bumblebees,
While the gopher steals peas with ease.
The sun winks down at this little show,
As flowers gossip, stretching to grow!

A robin sings, not quite in tune,
Trying to impress the glorious moon.
Squirrels tumble, with acorns galore,
Waging war, a nutty uproar!

Among the buds, laughter can sprout,
Nature's jesters, there's no doubt.
In stillness lies a playful spree,
Where silliness grows like the tallest tree!

Ballet of Blossoms in the Breeze

Daisies twirl in a floral ballet,
While dandelions prance all day.
Their pirouettes, a sight to behold,
With roots so stubborn and stories old!

Tulips wear tutus, bright and bold,
Wondering why they're not sold.
A daffodil strikes a silly pose,
Swaying gently, striking a rose!

The breeze conducts this merry show,
With laughter rippling, high and low.
Every petal has its own little part,
In this wacky, whimsical garden art!

At dusk, they bow, that's the cue,
A shower of pollen, a grand debut.
Underneath the twilight's tease,
They dream of silliness in the breeze!

A Place for the Wandering Soul

In the meadows where critters roam,
A lost sock finds its way back home.
With whispering winds and a playful glance,
Every wanderer joins the dance!

Ants march in a tiny parade,
Helping lost breadcrumbs find shade.
A frog in a top hat gives a cheer,
For every misplaced sock that wanders near!

Clouds drift by on a lazy day,
As mice gossip in their cheeky way.
In this nook of joy, paths interlace,
Where silly souls find their happy place!

With laughter echoing near and wide,
Under moonlight, with pride, they glide.
In the laughter of stars that twinkle and shine,
They makeup tales, oh, how they intertwine!

Solitude Beneath the Stars

Alone beneath the evening's glow,
A cactus wearing a sombrero!
It watches ants waltz up and down,
In this splendid, pinprick town!

A lone owl hoots a silly tune,
Swapping whispers with a quiet moon.
Stars blink and giggle in delight,
As fireflies flicker, a dazzling sight!

Wishing upon a marshmallow cloud,
The night wears a smile, oh so proud.
Silly shadows stretch and sway,
As the sun prepares for another day!

In solitude, where laughter entwines,
Every creature giggles, life defines.
Beneath the stars, hearts grow bold,
Finding joy in what nature unfolds!

Whispering Winds of Solace

In the breeze, I toss my hat,
A sneaky bird takes it for a spat.
I chase it down, what a sight,
A dance with feathers, a ridiculous fight.

The leaves giggle as they sway,
I trip on roots, oh what a day!
The whispers of trees teach me to fall,
While squirrels argue, I laugh with them all.

With every turn, I lose my grin,
But the grass is soft, let joy begin!
The wind blows secrets, oh so spry,
I join the gossip, just you and I.

So here I am, a fool of glee,
With nature's jokes, I'm wild and free.
The sun peeks through, and so I bow,
To the comic relief of life's plow!

Sunbeams Through the Canopy

Sunlight tickles the leaves with cheer,
I squint and grin, oh dear, oh dear!
The shadows play hide and seek with me,
I trip on laughter, oh how silly!

A rabbit hops past, with no care,
It's a fashion show, an auburn hare.
The sunbeams wink, they play along,
With every giggle, nature sings a song.

Mushrooms pop up, like tiny hats,
I join their party, they chatter like brats.
The daisies chuckle, all in good fun,
As I sway with the flowers, feeling like one.

So on I dance, where shadows glow,
In this wacky world, I steal the show.
With sun-kissed moments, and mirthful glee,
I'll frolic forever, just let me be!

Awakened by the Earth's Breath

A yawn escapes from the soft dawn grass,
I stumble out, sleep won't let me pass.
The earth's warm hug, it pulls me back,
But the smell of pancakes calls from the crack!

Footsteps crunch on the frosty ground,
Nature's alarm clock is a silly sound.
A crow caws out like a broken tune,
While I chase the sun, a sleepy cartoon.

The flowers bloom with whimsy cheer,
They want to tickle my toes, oh dear!
Each petal whispers, "don't be a bore,"
Join the fun and dance some more!

With roots and shoots in a silly game,
I trip and tumble, yet feel no shame.
So here I venture, with laughter anew,
The earth's breath chuckles, while I rendezvous!

Chasing Shadows of Silence

Shadows skitter across the glade,
They play tricks on me, a sneaky charade.
I give them chase, they giggle and flee,
I must be the jester, in a grand spree!

The grass whispers tales of playful jest,
While crickets chirp, they know me best.
With every leap, I trip on a breeze,
And ducks in the pond all laugh with ease.

The sun plays peekaboo behind the trees,
It giggles on branches, fluttering leaves.
"Catch me if you can!" it beams with glee,
And I become part of its comedy!

So in this chase, I find my bliss,
With shadows and laughter, how could I miss?
I'll twirl in silence, as jokes abound,
In this whimsical journey, joy is found!

Whispers of Tranquil Fields

In fields so vast, the grass takes flight,
A cow jumps high, what a silly sight!
The butterflies dance, or perhaps they prance,
While bees hum tunes in a goofy trance.

The daisies giggle, the thistles tease,
But who will win in the garden tease?
A squirrel with acorns, a hat on his head,
Claims he's the king of this poppy bed.

The sun winks low, a blushing light,
As worms in tuxedos twist with delight.
The clouds above float, they seem to grin,
While ants in a line march, hoping to win.

So here we frolic, with laughter so bright,
In the fields where joy takes its flight.
Amidst the giggles, and antics so true,
Nature's own stand-up, just for me and you.

Threads of Peaceful Blooms

In gardens of laughter, petals do sway,
With tulips debating who won yesterday.
The roses, so regal, in pranks they engage,
While sneaky old daisies turn the next page.

A sunflower, tall, plays peek-a-boo,
Saying boldly, "Well, I outgrew you!"
The bees, they buzz in a chaotic spree,
Claiming they're superheroes, can't you see?

The violets whisper, "Pass the sweet jam,"
While pansies chuckle, "We're all in this jam!"
A worm in a tie orders pizza for all,
While crickets recite verse, standing so tall.

Here in this garden, where fun never ends,
Each bloom shares laughter, and joy transcends.
With friendships abloom, and humor that flies,
In this colorful realm, happiness lies.

The Garden of Still Waters

By the pond quite still, the frogs start to croak,
As dragonflies chuckle at each funny joke.
The laughter echoes, ripples dance wide,
While turtles debate who's in charge of the tide.

The cattails sway, giving sage advice,
While goldfish giggle, "It's really quite nice!"
They tell funny tales of what they have seen,
In the quiet of waters, where all's evergreen.

Little ducks quack out a comedy show,
Waddling funny, with a splash and a glow.
While willows bow low, a graceful ballet,
The breeze whispers low, "Let's frolic and play!"

So here at the water, where giggles stay bright,
Nature's comedy spills, a delightful sight.
In the calm of the ripples, laughter does bloom,
Creating a haven, dispelling all gloom.

Petals Beneath a Quiet Sky

Under a canopy of blue candy floss,
A turtle in shades is the jester, the boss.
The daisies conspire for a silly parade,
With buttercups wearing their bold masquerade.

The clouds float by with a giggle, you see,
Trading fun secrets with the bumblebee.
The sun starts to smirk, cooling down for a rest,
While shadows stretch long, they compete for the best.

A rabbit on stilts hops past with a grin,
Claiming he's off to the next "best-dressed" win.
The grass, oh-so-green, rolls around in delight,
As squirrels toss acorns, oh what a sight!

Beneath this vast sky, where humor is sown,
Joy blooms in the petals, never alone.
With laughter and wonder, we're free as a kite,
In this whimsical garden, our hearts take flight.

The Serenity of Unseen Moments

In the quiet of the yard, I heard a sound,
A squirrel on a mission, so profound.
He paused mid-chase, and gave a wink,
As if to say, "You're overthinking!"

Bees buzzing softly, doing their dance,
While I try to catch them—ain't that a chance?
They buzz and zigzag, I trip on a shoe,
And ponder if honey's worth all this ado.

A caterpillar's pondering life on a leaf,
"I'll fly one day!" that's beyond disbelief.
But first a nap that lasts through the night,
A lazy ambition, oh what a sight!

Birds chirp in gossip, exchanging their news,
While I sip my coffee, reading the blues.
Nature's so funny, it's all in good cheer,
Moments of laughter—just bring your best beer!

Lush Layers of Reflection

In a garden where the gnomes seem to prance,
I spotted a frog lead a waltzy romance.
He croaked out a tune, so suave and so bold,
That nearby daisies began to unfold.

With layers of hues, blossoms burst into chat,
Discussing how rabbits play hopscotch like that.
A discreet little bee, gathering brunch,
Buzzing by, saying, "Volunteer for the lunch!"

Overhead, clouds rolled, fluffed up like a cake,
A squirrel observed, thinking, "How much to take?"
In this wild buffet of the garden so bright,
Even the weeds seem to throw a delight.

As shadows lengthen, the evening gets still,
Fireflies join in for their dance and their thrill.
With laughter and lights, they twinkle away,
While I'm here smirking at another fine day!

Boughs of Tranquility

Under a tree with branches so wide,
I come to a squirrel, who looks quite snide.
"You think you own this whole patch of shade?"
He flicks his tail, a little charade.

The breeze makes the leaves giggle with glee,
Telling secrets like, "Where's that guy with the tree?"
While a dog nearby sniffs at the air,
Wishing he could join the branch-chatter affair.

A raccoon rolls in, wearing pajamas so chic,
He swears he's an expert on hide-and-seek.
But with sleepy owls yawning so loud,
Even he knows it's best to be cowed.

With every rustle, a laugh shared by all,
Leaves cascade down like a playful soft fall.
You never know where the humor may sprout,
In the arms of the woods, let joy twist about!

Timeless Whispers of the Woods

In the woods where whispers cause giggles to stir,
The trees gossip tales; they always concur.
A bear hums a tune, out under the moon,
And says, "I just can't resist this sweet prune!"

Owls sharing puns, all wise and profound,
"Who's there?" they hoot, circling 'round.
The mushrooms chuckle, holding their ground,
As squirrels perform with acorns unbound.

Each rustle a riddle, each branch holds a jest,
While chipmunks debate who's the very best guest.
In nature's own laughter, companionship thrives,
Echoing mischief, where whimsy derives.

So join in the mirth, don't let it be shy,
Dance under the starlight, give joy a try.
For in the woods' laughter, life's beauty is seen,
Crafted in moments, both silly and keen!

When Time Paused for a Breath

The clock decided to take a nap,
Loudly snoring, no time to tap.
Tick-tock turned to tick-tock-snooze,
Moments shuffled in silly shoes.

We danced with shadows, quite the sight,
Chasing giggles under soft moonlight.
Laughter echoed through the trees,
As squirrels joined in with utmost ease.

A butterfly laughed at a sloth, so fast,
While birds played fetch, oh what a blast!
Time paused a moment, then said, "Alright!"
And we all fell asleep, what a night!

Waking up to a sunbeam's tease,
We stretched and yawned with perfect ease.
As clocks began to tick once more,
We shrugged and laughed, who keeps score?

Serene Reflections on Still Waters

A pond so calm, a glassy grin,
Where frogs wear crowns and fish swim in.
The ducks all waddle, what a show,
And lily pads applaud, 'Bravo!'

Reflections giggle, play hide and seek,
With every splash, a new little peek.
The ripples sing a soft, sweet song,
While turtles whisper, 'What's taking long?'

A dragonfly throws a dance party,
With moves so smooth, it feels quite hearty.
While moorhens drum without a care,
The evening mist floats, fills the air.

As shadows stretch, we wave goodbye,
To the water's mirror, under the sky.
With laughter echoing, a tranquil cheer,
Where every moment is pure and clear.

Threads of Calm in Nature's Tapestry

In the garden, the flowers weave,
A blanket soft with tales to believe.
Bees buzz jokes, flowers giggle loud,
While daisies dance, feeling quite proud.

A wind that's playful, twirls with grace,
Tickles the leaves in a charming race.
Butterflies gossip, soaring high,
About a squirrel, oh, my, oh my!

The sun peeks in with a cheeky wink,
While shadows gather to share a drink.
The grass tickles toes, oh what fun!
Under the laughter of the bright sun.

In this tapestry of silly threads,
Nature smiles, as joy spreads.
We laugh along, a carefree crew,
In harmony's quilt, stitched anew.

The Language of Quiet Blooms

Among the petals, secrets are shared,
In whispers soft, no need to be scared.
Tulips trip over daisies' hats,
While pansies giggle, how fun is that?

A bee wrote a book, a buzzed-out tome,
Filled with tales of flowers at home.
The moss giggles softly, hiding beneath,
As vines poke fun from their leafy sheath.

At twilight's touch, the blooms conspire,
Sharing stories by the glow of fire.
As crickets chatter, night becomes bright,
With moonbeam laughter, all feels right.

Each petal speaks in colors bold,
A canvas of joy, a sight to behold.
In the garden's heart, laughter is found,
Where silly blooms spread joy all around.

A Veil of Peace Over the Landscape

In fields of green, a big cow sings,
With flowers dressed in silly rings.
They dance around without a care,
Tickling bees, a buzzing square.

The sun peeks in, a cheeky grin,
And daisies laugh at where they've been.
The clouds play tag above the hills,
Sharing secrets, thrilling chills.

A breeze rolls through with jokes to tell,
As butterflies spell words so well.
In this bouquet of giggling blooms,
Serious woes just fade and fume.

So frolic forth, let laughter swell,
In nature's arms, all is quite well.
With each soft laugh, the heart takes flight,
In peace, we find our silly light.

The Hidden Sanctuary of the Soul

Beneath the leaves, a squirrel naps,
Dreaming of acorns and silly mishaps.
A snail gets lost, slow as a phrase,
In its shell, it counts the days.

A wise old owl spins tales of yore,
While crickets chirp their nightly score.
They weave a charm, a soothing tune,
Inviting dreams under the moon.

Here, troubles bounce like bouncy balls,
As laughter dances in these halls.
With twinkling eyes and joy in tow,
Nature's humor steals the show.

So, take a seat on mossy stones,
Exchange your woes, your weary tones.
In this refuge where giggles reign,
Find the peace amidst the plain.

Moonlit Pathways of Solitude

A moonbeam slips and trips on roots,
Frogs jump high in silly hoots.
The path is lit by twinkling stars,
That tease the shadows, play with scars.

A lone raccoon in silver light,
Holds a disco ball, ready for night.
Whispers echo, a playful game,
In solitude, it's not the same.

Crickets wear tiny top hats tight,
As fireflies dance with sheer delight.
Here in the quiet, there's always fun,
Even the night wishes to run.

So wander forth without a care,
Join the laughter that fills the air.
In moonlit pathways, let joy unfold,
A cozy tale that's never old.

The Serenade of Enchanted Glades

In grassy clearings where rabbits chat,
They ponder life, discuss the fat.
A hedgehog strums a twiggy lute,
Performing tunes that shake the root.

The trees sway gently to the beat,
Sharing secrets, oh so sweet.
A chorus of birds sings loud and bright,
In enchanted glades, there's pure delight.

A breeze fluffs feathers, tickles noses,
While daisies play peek-a-boo with roses.
Laughter bubbles like a brook,
In nature's arms, all woes are shook.

So join the dance, let worries cease,
In woodland halls, we find our peace.
With every note, the heart takes wing,
In this sweet serenade, joy takes spring.

Peaceful Paths Less Traveled

There once was a goat with a hat,
He pondered the world, and just sat.
He'd munch on some leaves,
With the humming of bees,
While dreaming of cheese, oh imagine that!

The trails off the beaten, he'd roam,
With squirrels who called him their home.
They'd giggle and dance,
In a silly prance,
As they planned their great journey to gnome.

A rabbit on stilts waved hello,
With a wink and a flip of his toe.
The goat let out bleats,
As he made funny beats,
And they laughed at the clouds, nice and low.

So if you find paths not in view,
Join the laughs and the smiles, that's the cue.
With friends in the trees,
Life's a soft breeze,
In a world that feels friendly and new!

Elysian Echoes

In fields where the daisies all grin,
Lived a chicken with dreams of a win.
She danced on one leg,
With a humorous beg,
To join in the fun and the din.

A pig with a crown joined the tease,
He thought he could dance, if you please.
With his wobble so grand,
He drew quite the band,
While causing a ruckus of sneeze.

The ducks quacked in rhythm so sweet,
Their laughter made everyone beat.
As they paraded by,
Underneath the blue sky,
All forgot of their worries, what a treat!

As echoes of giggles took flight,
In the meadows where all felt so right.
They spun round and round,
With joy that they found,
In a frolicsome world, pure delight!

The Soft Glow of Dusk

The sun waved goodbye with a grin,
While fireflies flickered to win.
A cat and a mouse,
Slightly lost in their house,
Played peek-a-boo games in the din.

As shadows crept in from the west,
The laughter stirred up from the nest.
With a leap and a bound,
They discovered a sound,
Of crickets who thought they were best.

The dog joined the fun in a chase,
While the hedgehog spun round in place.
"Oh dear!" was the shout,
As they spun all about,
In a blur of sheer joy and grace.

With dusk casting hues of delight,
The world danced away from the night.
In the glow, hearts were warm,
In the soft sunset charm,
Where laughter released every fright.

Restorative Rhythms of Twilight

At twilight, the crickets arrive,
Singing tunes that help us survive.
A hedgehog in socks,
Did circle the clocks,
While crafting a dance that's alive.

The bats chime in, swooping low,
Adding flair to the evening's great show.
With a flap and a cheer,
They brought friends ever near,
To join in the wild and the glow.

A raccoon with a hat made of leaves,
Taught the others how to gather eves.
With a wiggle and twirl,
He spun round like a girl,
Enthralled by the quirkiest thieves.

As night draped its blanket, we laughed,
Shared stories of fun that were daft.
With rhythm so bright,
Through the magical night,
We danced until dreams were our craft.

Moments Slipping Through Gentle Fingers

In a garden where giggles bloom,
Time dances in a bright costume.
We chase shadows, just like light,
And trip on laughter, what a sight!

Teacups spill while stories grow,
Butterflies join the cheeky show.
Jellybeans fall from the sky,
As we munch and giggle, oh my!

The clock's a joker, tickles a beat,
Each moment's a prank, oh what a treat!
With every second, we play a trick,
Time slips by, so smooth and quick.

So here we are, with snacks in hand,
Spinning through fun, just as we planned.
In a whirl of joy, our hearts take flight,
Moments like candy, oh what delight!

Silhouettes of Tranquility in the Twilight

As dusk wraps up a cheeky day,
The sky paints jokes in the twilight sway.
Clouds wear hats, and stars wear shoes,
While the sun takes bows and bids adieu.

Crickets chirp a funny tune,
While fireflies dance with the moon.
Shadows play hide and seek with the breeze,
In this quiet, we giggle with ease.

Whispers float like bubbles in air,
Tickling senses, beyond compare.
In silhouettes, we find our fun,
With laughter echoed 'neath the setting sun.

A gentle hush blankets the scene,
As silly dreams begin to convene.
In twilight's laugh, our spirits gleam,
We find delight in this twilight dream.

Whispers in the Meadow

In a meadow where daisies tumble,
Funny whispers make us stumble.
A breeze tells jokes in a playful tone,
While butterflies giggle on their own.

We chase the clouds with silly glee,
As pigs play tag, oh can't you see?
The grass tickles our toes so fine,
In this wild world, we sip sweet wine.

Sunny spots become our stage,
Where nonsense lines break every cage.
Rabbits wear glasses, and cows do the jig,
Life here is wacky, there's always a gig!

So come along to dance and play,
In such a meadow, worries sway.
With whispers of joy and laughter's call,
We'll find our peace, the best of all!

Gentle Echoes of Calm

In the stillness, echoes of glee,
Tickled by breezes, come dance with me.
The trees sway slow, with laughter's grace,
While nature winks, a funny face.

Ripples giggle on a quiet brook,
As frogs in suits read a silly book.
Crickets wear glasses, tune in the show,
With every note, our smiles grow.

Clouds debate on a game of chess,
While squirrels wear masks, it's pure finesse.
Leaves rustle softly, sharing a laugh,
In this gentle calm, we take a bath.

So join the echoes of quiet delight,
Where laughter twirls in the soft moonlight.
In this calm, with joy we engage,
Finding fun on every page!

www.ingramcontent.com/pod-product-compliance
Lightning Source LLC
Chambersburg PA
CBHW051633160426
43209CB00004B/622